DREAM DUST

Born in Portadown, Northern Ireland, **Marcus Silcock** (formerly Slease) has made his home in Turkey, Poland, Italy, South Korea, the United States, Spain, and the United Kingdom – experiences that inform his surreal-absurd travel writing. He co-edits surreal-absurd for Mercurius magazine. His poetry has been translated into Turkish, Slovakian, Polish, and Danish. He is the author of *Never Mind the Beasts* (Dostoyevsky Wannabe), *The Green Monk* (Boiler House Press), and *Play Yr Kardz Right* (Dostoyevsky Wannabe), among others. Currently, he lives in Sitges and teaches high school in Barcelona. Find out more at: Never Mind the Beasts (www.nevermindthebeasts.com)

As Marcus Slease

Puppy   (Beir Bua Press, 2021)

Never Mind the Beasts   (Dostoyevsky Wannabe, 2020)

The Green Monk   (Boiler House Press, 2018)

The Spirit of the Bathtub   (Apocalypse Party, 2018)

Play Yr Kardz Right   (Dostoyevsky Wannabe, 2017)

Rides   (Blart Books, 2014)

Paddy's Cure (with Pascal O'Loughlin)   (Deadwood Press, 2014)

The House of Zabka   (Deathless Press, 2013)

Elephanche (with SJ Fowler)   (deptpress, 2013)

Hello Tiny Bird Brain   (Knives Forks and Spoons Press, 2012)

Mu (Dream) So (Window)   (Poor Claudia, 2012)

Godzenie   (Blazevox Books, 2009)

PRAISE for *Dream Dust*

In the grand tradition of prose poems, Marcus Silcock's delightful *Dream Dust* is surreal, for sure, but in a way that complements rather than covers up the truth. Personal recollections and strong narrative undertones lie just below the bright, windy surface. These charming fictions take place all over the world but their subject is always what it looks like to be fully human, to be fully present, wherever you happen to be. *Dream Dust* makes a fine traveling companion.
— Matthew Rohrer

Marcus Silcock's newest collection, *Dream Dust*, is a masterful assemblage of prose poems. Are they autobiographical surrealisms or surrealist autobiographies? You decide. From Vegas to Seoul to Sitges to Wrocław, here we have a cosmic trip disguised as an international voyage. Prose poems with heart and dilated pupils. Tender yet absurd. Hallucinatory and strange, twirling through a fable, like taking psychedelics in the American desert and waking up in a Polish forest. Instead of a spaghetti western, this is a pierogi fever dream. This unique collection is full of forests and beer steins and cultural ceremonies and Eastern European architecture and magic broth. It's global, musical, and nostalgic every step of the way, like finding a tattered diary in a bowl of borscht. "You can count the tree rings on my forehead," Silcock promises us, later stating, "I am surrendering to this experience." We believe him and so we do the same. Through it all, *Dream Dust* is packed with sharp, punchy memories. Scraps of the past splashed in a foggy dew. If you try to find your way through these riveting narratives, know the compass is spinning and the map has caught fire. To open this book is to "roll the bone dice" and begin a new game. Give it a shot. See where you land.
— Ben Niespodziany

Dream Dust is an encyclopaedia of peculiarities and particularities. The title piece begins: 'This place is famous for shits and giggles.' These prose poems or micro-narratives are typically laconic; not infrequently metaphysical and/or philosophical. 'How uninteresting interesting things can become,' said Robert Walser', the German Swiss poet known as 'the poet of miniatures'.

Dream Dust is supple and ludic and deadpan and serious and invigorating and comic. In quasi-Swiftian mode we find ourselves stumbling upon 'Giant metal babies crawling with their metal bums in the air.' Seemingly, '[t]hose metallic bums were the future.' The book signs off with 'Hungry Ghosts'. The speaker follows 'the white monkey (Biała Małpa) down the hole and into the beer garden.' A little later 'Someone smiles. Miles & miles of good smile.'
— Julian Stannard

CONTENTS

I

II

ISBN: 978-1-916938-84-7

Cover designed by Aaron Kent

Edited and Typeset by Aaron Kent

Broken Sleep Books Ltd
PO BOX 102
Llandysul
SA44 9BG

Dream Dust

Marcus Silcock

Broken Sleep Books

I

WOLFSON

In Warrington, father sheared sheep. His brother raced
greyhounds. They watched John Wayne on the telly. It is hard to
imagine now, but a lucky coin behind the ear meant something.
Father followed those coins to Vallejo California. The trailer park.
We all lived there. Hamburger Helper. I can still taste it. Also, *The
Fall Guy*, with Lee Majors. That opening theme song was my life
song. Lots of doubles. Behind the scenes. Plus bounty hunting
even though I didn't know what I was hunting. Then it was Vegas.
Toothpicks, steak and eggs for 2 dollars, and a donated Nova.
Father with angel dust and sneaky pokes with Cheryl. Then it
was small-town Utah. By then, father had changed his accent
to cowboy western. Two horses snorted me. Vultures circled
the dusty fields. Tussling through the night with angels, claws
scraping our ears. Every morning, the town crier shook the bell.
The end was nigh. One day, father went deep into a new cult. He
lived in a shack outside someone's house, white sheets covering
his windows, dead animals in the trees to ward off evil spirits.
I shook the dust from my shoes, an ancient curse. I was leaving
behind the fellowship of the kingdom. Tainted. I leaked my guts.
Slouched from one country to another. Searching for something.
Shearing my sheep wool. Pulling out my wolf daggers. Trying to
avoid father.

THE DREARY DAYS OF DICKY BOWS

The guests arrived. They stuck me in the olive green army cot.
Father broke out the pork chops. The guests gathered around
and I sat in the middle. They fired up their hands to reign down
holy spirits. I bloomed in the dark. I lay on my side thinking of
doubting Thomas. His index finger in the raw flesh of Jesus. I
knuckled my fingers into deep prayer position. Pressed my knees
beneath trees for new visions. The passing truck headlights were
avenging angels. At mother's wedding the dreary dicky bow. It
was hard to breathe in there. Suddenly we were immigrating. The
missionaries sponsored us for America. Trailer park with gumball
machine. How do you float a bubble. I wet my feet on white paper
to see their shape. Long thin ships to sail outta here.

KISSES CAUSE CAVITIES

For so long, dreaming of it. Watching those German film strips.
Opening the escape hatch into cold war Germany. I am not
German but German brings me warm feelings. I slip into my
loin cloth. Drink my coffee. Finally going, I say. Outside the
train station, we head for the Späti. Everyone is baggy. Baggy is
back. I grew up with baggy, I say. Back at the hotel, we bounce
the bed. Splurge this, says Marcin, lifting the Egyptian sheets
into the wind. Boiled eggs for breakfast. Drip coffee. We are
staying in Mitte, but wander east for East City Wall graffiti. 99
Luftballons lift me into alternative eighties. Ghetto blaster on my
shoulder. Gosia leans into the boutique ice cream at Checkpoint
Charlie. Imagine this deathstrip. Imagine this river crossing.
At Krautsberg, piercing ear with small black triangle, buying a
yolk yellow cap. We sit down at the cafe. The wasps fierce and
relentless. Put the orange from your Aperol on the other table,
says Marcin, maybe the wasps will leave us. We delve into Turkish
meze. Anarchist squat flags wave at us. At Humboldt Forum,
happy DJs. Everyone out there in open air with polite spaces
between us. Waving our arms. Shaking our shoulders and hips.
Wrestling with thorny histories. Statues, streets, squares, who
cares. In the crowded marketplace of identities, you slip out of
one skin into another. Kisses cause cavities. Weeping willows
bend down to touch you. Half moon fingernail snags the peaches.

EVERYTHING IS A RELIC OF SOMETHING

After a day of drenching, we slide into the carriage to Wrocław.
The carriages are filled with young people from the 1960s. Shaggy
hair and baggy clothing. They are traveling to the largest free
festival in Poland. What does this age demand? How is it different
than the last one? Everything is a relic of something. You can
count the tree rings on my forehead. Last night my friend was
small slice of brain sludging blood on ground with no mouth to
speak. You cannot lose too much lifeblood. I was trying to return
him to his body. Your brain is part of your body. Your heart sends
messages. It is also the control centre. In the east, the seat of
consciousness is in the chest. The heart. But in the west it's the
head. I'd like to be here, you say, tapping your chest. But I think
I'm here, you say, tapping your temples.

PARROTS

Beach herders flop their flip flops in November. This is the land of scorched earth. Sin sinks into the loins. Flogging, beating, branding, mutilation, blinding, and the use of the stock and pillory. We've mostly moved past that (hopefully). Down the road on sin street you enter Parrots. The waiters all wear bright clothing. You sit on chairs facing the street watching the colourful people pass by you. A little bright umbrella in your cocktail and straw hat on your head. I'm not one for the parrots. My face is full of ghost sheets. Dreaming of northern countries. Where the light expires early. Where winter sweeps the streets of people into cosy corners. Those crackling fires. Warm wine. The trees stripped down to their original colours. The air nips your skin in northern countries. The lights light up your inner life in northern countries. Dreaming of dreamy pumpkins with romantic candles. The fields nipped with frost. The crunch sound is your favourite sound. The interior lives of inner lives spread across the northern hillsides.

REPUBLIC

All of us out there. Bundles of personalities. Morn noon and
night. All shapes & sizes. Some little rebels. Some natural herders
or bird fluffers. Rock chasers & tunnellers. Middle age thrusters.
We don't own anything. We don't want to own anything, but in
this country you have to own something. If you want to survive
old age without family. 60,000 down. We'll never get there. We
can keep playing the lottery. Pushing our luck. Or maybe we will
never make it to retirement age. How do people stop working and
still eat? The spinach and mushrooms taste like old shoe polish.
The air biting. That means you have to move faster. Jaunts around
the town. Rapping wooden planks with knuckles. You work and
work to make the rich people richer. Liberty equality fraternity.
There is a long way to go there. The republic of consciousness.
The republic of eyes. The republic of lies. The republic of fears.
The republic of shadows dancing there behind your eyes.

PULSE OF THE NATION

The old radio plays music from the Weimar Republic. The tubas like old frogs. The rats in the alley alive but muffled. Outside: one big fog. It feels like something with fangs is coming for you. A little bit Dracula. Suddenly the phone rings. And then another. The streets are full of phone booths. The phone booths are clouded. But here and there, like departing clouds, the light shines inside. You can see the brief outlines. People cradling telephones. Rocking slowly. What is the pulse of the nation? It is growing quicker. The enemies of the people are multiplying. The department of justice sends hawks from the sky to nab you.

SHOVEL

Keep shovelling. & shovelling. & shovelling. I stand on my
balcony. Lads across the way at the pub. Come on down. It is
always someone's birthday. Midnight vodka with pickled herring.
Walking past the baker boy with his famous shovel, I feel heroic.
What a shovel! Saving the town from Teutonic knights. The world
is full of shovels. The coal shovel for the fireplace. The trench
shovel for deep hidings. The cement shovel for new walls. We
live in the 21st century. We shovel shit into us. Take the wooden
handle of the shovel. Keep shovelling. & shovelling. & shovelling.
Maybe someday you will get there.

TANGERINE DREAMS

We chummed around Mitte district. Soaked in the street art. Feathered our ears with new sounds at the record shop. But outside there was a crowd gathering. We went outside to find someone covered in fishnets. Fishnet sewed their mouth shut. Cans of empty beer circled around them as they snaked and spasmed on the ground. Someone moved closer to see them. Should we help them, said one. I don't think it's human, said another. Someone call someone, said someone. That person is probably in trouble. It is not human, said another. And another. We all moved closer. Something was mumbling in those fishnets. The movements were robotic. The radio in the corner was from the 70s. It is probably an art exhibit, said someone. No, it's a real person, said another. We kept looking. The mouth swung open and then closed in the fishnets.

HOPSCOTCH

I am always hoping to move ahead. I yell out my next moves.
Teeth, I yell, before brushing them. Rubbish, I yell, before
running with dripping sack toward bins. Everyone knows the big
bang. Now there is the big crunch, big freeze, big crumble, but
my favourite is the big bounce. I bounced into childhood with my
stone washed jeans. Oh stud muffins. Oh watery ketchup & chalky
curry powder. Berlin blinks into the future. "How uninteresting
interesting things can become" said Robert Walser. We are all
dead already. No future. Reality in a nutshell and fear in a handful
of dust. All dusty dream glitter.

WHITE ELEPHANTS

We searched for the biggest medieval square on the map. The biggest medieval square was not really a medieval square. It was a green park devoid of the flaky textures of medieval buildings. No buggy and cart. No old cloth market twinkling in amber. We walked around the green hills. There was something metallic in the distance. Giant metal babies crawling with their metal bums in the air. Can you feel it, said Agata. The air was changing around us. Those metallic bums were the future. We walked through them. Down in the beer bunkers we could revive. Can-can dancers can-canned their way around the tables. Beer foam matted the beer mats. We are really living, I said. The can-can dancers parted ways. They carted the kitchen sink onto the stage. Pitched pennies. It's underground cabaret, said Agata. It is full of surprises. A hat, a shawl, a lit candle. The simple gesture of raising the hands. I am surrendering to this experience, I said, raising my hands up and down. Moving away from modern pressures. No longer bedding down with debts of ownership. I felt the animal hairs hugging my body. All these animals dreaming. Legs and eyelids twitching. Mouth moving soundless in dead of night. How the days of our lives bleed us, bless us, drown us, carry us, cramp us, suffer us. This cabaret of arrows shot through the throat of the hourly trumpet blower. This cabaret of love machines humming in the distance. This cabaret of organs pipping out their fleshy whistles. Coins clank in my pockets. Mild strikes. Heavenly music. White elephants.

THE GREEN TICKET

The whistle blows the midnight train. Two seater. Plenty of toe space. Green fields rolling in the wind out the window. Suddenly lots of fairy lights lighting up water under bridges. I hand my green ticket to the conductor and he stamps my hand for the field dance. We pour mammalian milk into the lip of the flower. Lola chomps at bees but we don't want her to swallow one. Today we learn to lick ice cream. Stick out your tongue and turn the cone round and round into tight circles. Soft tongue. Soft tongue. That's why they have the best lovers in these parts.

DEER IN THE BEER

The foam in my beer swirls into an ancient cave painting. There's a deer in my beer, says the goth. The goth is romantic. Yelps of dogs in foggy green fields. Musty scent. She wants to migrate away from the big hungry money grab. It is called housing crisis. It is called cost of living crisis. I don't bite my nails but cut them crooked, says the goth. They grow back sharp and jagged. In the kitchen magic broth beckons. She sips the magic broth. She counts the holy sheep across waves of sleep. Here she is now. Walking land as flat as pancakes. The nether regions of her heart's content. She looks for bicycles, but no bicycles. Even the bicycles are asleep. The mighty deers suck the berries of tomorrow. The mighty deers stick their eyes thru the keyhole. The mighty deers kindle in love a wantonness. The mighty deers smile with all their teeth. The mighty deers flicker.

UNDERGROUND

Deep in the belly of the city, we meet the musicians, from French
Quebec. It is only 5 euro. Little pops & bleeps. Crashing cymbals.
Brushing the drums & breathing. Wailing into walls of sound.
Francois Carrier & Michel Lambert. Francois on saxophone.
Michel on drums. We chat with them during intermission. In
Cork it was very intense, says Michel. So many levels. Boatloads
of Murphy's. It's the Cork version of Guinness, says Eimear. Yes,
says Michel, making a small smack with his lips. We were just in
Poland, says Michel. Rumia, Poznań & Gdansk. Terrific, I say.
I liked the pierogi, says Michel. Not at first. The first pierogi was
too slimy, but I thought I had to try another one. The other one
was very tasty. You have to have the right pierogi, I say. Have you
tried Katowice, I say, my hometown. I've heard about it, says
Michel. I've a friend, the head of the jazz department. I keep
meaning to visit. It is a good city for the underground, even
if the avant-garde is very small, I say. It is small by definition,
says Michel. We sit down for part two. Saxophone, drums, &
two local musicians, Diego Caicedo and Pablo Schvarzman,
on electric guitars. I close my eyes. Primeval energies. Walls of
sound. Swaying my head. The breathy valves. Rising & falling.
Michel cuts his finger on the high hat. The electric guitar moves
into space operas as he exits the stage for a bandage behind the
bar. Francois scrapes a square piece of plastic on the floor. I
needed that, I say.

MONO NO AWARE

Upon the streets we doth tread. Grey after grey until we stumble upon Holy Tavern. Pilgrims and wanderers. The board lists the special. The outside wooden table heaving. We slip down the alley and sit on the ancient church bench. Your finger is a stinky finger pointing at the moon. Look in the mirror. The mockingbird sings inside there. Mono No Aware. That slender sadness squeezing through the gap in the door. Mono No Aware. The body of sausage salted with time. And so we roll the bone dice. Bang on, I say, tracing the deep ridge between my eyebrows. Bang on, I say, twisting my silver tooth for new signals.

COOK
(thank you Leonora Carrington and Salvador Dalí)

I've signed up for an evening class in cooking. Luciana from
upstairs is in the class with a ring of burns up and down her arms.
Cat balls on her jumper. Also Isabella. Her cherry covered apron
& lopsided smile. The cooking teacher has twinkling bracelets.
Pencil thin eyebrows. There are so many ways to make a pie. Wild
boar. Heavy on the cocoa powder. Melons stuffed with larks.
Horse carrots. Butterfly zucchinis. Crayfish in viking herbs. The
face has three functions: emotions, eating, and sweating. In your
dreams, the smells are absent.

HAZELNUT HEAVEN

The showers have been threatening since morning. At the veggie shop, the cherries are better for 1 kilo. She runs outside, into the rain, adds more cherries. They weigh it. It is not enough. She runs out into the rain, fills the plastic bag, more cherries, & more cherries, & more cherries. You can get a lot of cherries for 1 kilo. The luxury avocados are 2 euros. It is good with blended tomatoes and garlic. An animal smile wants to eat you. Eyeliner, smudged and smeared. A picket fence of teeth. Ageing, maturing, time ticking & ticking. She remembers South Kensington, French or upper class English, walled gardens and picnics. She was never at home among the fancy, the rich or the haughty. She was never at home in any nation or country. She balled her backpack, trekked north into the wilderness. The summer camp children are screaming, a green monster is coming to eat them. She treks it through the mini jungle, hacks its limbs with a machete. A fine powder for face painting. She is the hero of the children's adventure. There is a horse, slanted. Woodsmoke from a chimney. A tiny fridge full of chocolate. Hazelnut heaven!

STRANGER THINGS

Childhood and alcoholism. She was born to kill giants. What is the relation of shyness to appearance? She waves her arms into a windmill. The Spanish are prone to melodrama. Children's tacos. Heavy metal junkies. Funk to funky. It's time to cure the pickles. The ultimate aim of all love affairs is the greatest aim but how to aim it, and where. Jupiter is close to the moon and *Stranger Things* is on the television. Ben has broken his leg, it is 4000 to fix it, with a low percentage of success. He can manage with three legs but cannot wander outside. Ben is 16, already old. It is better to die happy than live miserably. Some men are told to find someone to complete themselves and also become somebody. Some women are told to find somebody but not become somebody. Some men are told to become somebody but not to find somebody. She is somebody first and can find anybody later, but when do you know when you are somebody enough to find anybody. What is the complete equation?

Somebody: My tiny feet have grown into my face
Anybody: The waves are my children
Somebody: The dragonfly follows the snake
Anybody: The cold watch ticks against my wrist
Somebody: The tired candle burns over my shoulder
Anybody: Cookies & cream in the glory hole

HOT CLOUDS!

We are out of tonic, she says, can we mix the gin with tap water. The tonic is down the street at Condis, but the temptations of crisps await them. Maybe a small bag, she says. It is hard to shake the hankering. Crisps, or the closely related chip, is hard to resist, the most addictive food on the planet. The comfort of a fried potato. How did Europe survive without it? There is the olive, the centre of the mediterranean diet, health and longevity. Crisps with olive oil are very tasty. In England, it was prawn cocktail, in Poland sour cream. Did the English invent the thick chip. A broad sword. The French the straw chip. A thin Musketeer. A crisp should be crispy on the outside, a hot cloud on the inside. It is hard to eat just one.

THEY DIDN'T FEEL SOVIET

In her youth, it was sailors, crusty beards in bars. She didn't drink her beer with a straw. The world was colder then- winter longer. Sledding down the hill on her estate, bottle cap games on pavements. Her mother worked in an office and her father investigated crooked cops. They took the number off the door for protection. Her father returned from trips to Germany with real chocolate. It was the Cold War and they didn't feel Soviet. She sailed out to sea with the sailors, every afternoon till evening.

GIRL & HORSE

She is a child, on a horse, in the photo, and the paper with the
image of her on the horse is ageing, the image is fading, both her
and the horse, and the picture of her on the horse, both of them
together, on the grass, in 1980s Poland, with the fences far in the
distance, the horse and her galloping, later, out of the picture, to
something new, the parting clouds of forgetting.

TODA PICA

What is the use of traveling? Mattresses on footpaths, some slashed, not to be used later, & then further down the road, pillows, todo pica, something has invaded, cover your mattress in salt, todo pica, something has invaded, get rid of standing water, do not invite them to harvest, spray white vinegar, hang chalk in your closet, peel a vegetable, there are so many cities but really it is one city, feeding in the evening, or early in the morning, something tickling you, in London, the daddy longlegs, a bathtub crawler, enough poison to kill you, but no jaw to bite you, in the desert of Vegas, black widows and scorpions, make sure to shake out your shoe.

II

FEATHERS IN YOUR CAP

When I lived in Seoul, my life was cake. There was even a swivel chair in my office. Not to mention a sink. It was bigger than my living space. I felt kind of important. Every day there were two options for lunch. Black bean sauce with rice or Korean pizza with hot sauce. Those were nice choices but after some time every nice choice becomes limited. On Fridays, I sat around the all-U-Can-Eat sushi buffet. That was a new thing for me. Watching those little fish boats sail by. After all that sushi, I felt the glow. It lasted for maybe two hours. Then my goshiwon with a tiny television spitting out gameshows. People walking planks and swallowing spiders. I thought yes. I've made it. I am really living the adventure. Then my new meds turned my hair orange. I kept looking out the window. I had the latest technology of 2006. A screen that moved up and down, and even horizontal and vertical. With all those angles I thought I was going to really find something. A man rang the buzzer and took the lift to my 14th floor. I didn't know what he wanted, but I trusted him. When he opened the door he handed me his pinky to shake. Before long we were meeting regularly. Near the river. And then other pinkies came along. We felt the pink spirit of punk. My meds ballooned my face. Turned my face pink. I couldn't sing a lick. The Pinkies left me. Flowers sprout without mouths, do you wish to speak to them? I began to incline my head towards visions of Poland. Riding this straw odyssey on bargain baskets wheeled by milk matrons on cobbled towns. A few feathers in your cap, but they fly away quickly.

THE BELLS OF CHEVRON

In my crustacean period, shaving my head and gorging on beef jerky. Smoking in the storage room, the manager sat on the milk crate and told me about horses. I listened to conspiracy radio. I worked the graveyard. The aliens were coming, had come, had left traces. A man came in every day, gave me a wink, left with a twelve pack. When he smoked, he rested the cigarette near his crotch with his thumb in the belt loop. A model came in every evening after her workout. She left with three Snickers and a pack of long thin cigarettes. I grew plumpish reading world mythology. I coated my tongue and spoke German. In my sleep, the bells kept dinging. I turned up the radio. It was full of metal. I left this job to sell satellites on the phones.

KONTROLLER

I was inside the old electric in Katowice, rattling & humming.
Everyone very serious. Kontroler, the people whispered. Some
people tried to squeeze out at the next stop, but kontroler
worked from the front and back. Squeezed you in the middle.
There was nowhere to go. I feel the pinch in the room with the
walls moving back & forth. I am being sucked into them. I try
to hold my breath. Stick my neck out to keep from suffocating.
Where were you going? I try to find my ticket. But there's no
ticket. Only fairy lint.

THE MASTER

Threadbare was the name of my childhood. Someone else was always pulling the strings. I've caught the string puller, said father, but there was always another string puller above us. Father pulled the strings to slip out of the British army. We landed in Vegas. We pulled the slots. Something came out of them. Then nothing. Here, said the missionary, no strings attached. You can become the god of many children. You can hang the chandeliers in your garden. You can live forever in the top level kingdom. We pulled some strings, but there was always more string pullers above us. We stroked the white stripe on our Starsky and Hutch car. Sold blah blah to our neighbours. We moved two squares ahead and four squares to the right. We were going somewhere. We kept pulling strings, but there was always more strings ahead of us, behind us, above us. Oh great string puller. You are the master of this universe.

DREAM DUST

This place is famous for shits and giggles. It's a real crapshoot throwing the dog ball. You never know where you land. Good luck they say if it splats you. Don't open yr mouth. You'll swallow too many midges. Something hard hits my forehead. Giant flying beetle. An eater of palms. What is your future? We have to dream bigger. Hippies working the crowd. Pulling randoms to the front with their balloon trousers. Performing their famous flop dance. The slugs of love. You could feel it in the air. There's animal surge everywhere. That's a good one, she says. Here's another one. Misty days. Whales snorting to Alaska. Libations and wicker baskets in Bellingham. Hemp hats and green glow. Drumming against the WTO in Seattle. That's not a dream, she says, it happened. Yes, I say, my dreams are all nostalgia. They are all in the past. Happened or not happened, I say. I'm 50. She's 40. We wait for a hamburger from Big Al's. The hamburger is late by a few decades. You are only honest in the bedroom, she says.

NAKED FREEDOM

Here in Sitges, the city of fiestas, leaning into your brave potatoes.
Air perfumed for the evening. An older lady, very animated,
comes towards you holding a pair of sandals. The young
shopkeeper is the translator. She asks you to try. Do you mind,
says the shopkeeper, pointing to the pair of sandals in the older
lady's hands. You try on the sandals & walk around the shop.
The older lady watches you. You become the strutter. No, says
the saleslady. She must see your feet. You remove the socks. You
become the naked sandal. You moved from one country known
for socks with their sandals to another country well known for
naked sandals. You moved to this country for naked freedom, but
you cannot shake the wearing of socks with your sandals.

SWAN SONGS

Bikinis at Café Slurp. Lithographs of Miró in the window. Trying
not to think of your lost thermals, your sour breath. Big lump
on the inside. Outside divine beanpole. Naked men and women
at Balmins beach. They've left their shame behind them. After
playing touch and go between this world and the great mystery
during emergency surgery, there was the after shock. A noun not
a verb. Someplace like a frozen lake. Or old wood petrified into
stone. Do you hear god's megaphone shouting out suffering to
wake up the deaf world? The deaf are blocks of stone, and god's
chisel (ouch!) chisels them into perfection. Or bends them low
to the earth like broken pineapples. Like swan songs in helium
balloons.

THE WAY

I'm in love with the foggy dew. Since that is my birthplace. Where
do you come from? The foggy dew. Where are you going? The
foggy few. Why are you here? The foggy dew. Money screams and
I can only walk. Smarmy creatures invade me. Nodding my head
till my neck aches. Curling into smoke to take less space on the
sidewalk. You can catch the wind in my sails on Sunday. Bouncing
the mop in the bedroom. Stacking hot potatoes into castles.
Surrounding them with milk moat. We are all haunted houses.
Smaller creatures eating bigger creatures. Bigger creatures eating
smaller creatures. Moving through the Milky Way. Eating each
other.

MEAT CURTAINS

So long working the night radio dreaming of flying saucers.
Saucy people live in saucy houses with lemon curtains. New
advances from Spain. My boots stretch with my toes. They are
scuffed but my toes ride freely in the toe box. There is also my
new Danish bag called Rains. A gift from fellow teacher who
also gifted me Gottfried Keller's Der grüne Heinrich. It will take
yonkers to plonk along in German. And now we doth delight in
our breakfast. Little waterlogged holes that reminds me of milk
teeth. Those were some days sitting around with toothless granny.
Kicking the can down the alley of burnt houses. Sometimes you
want to jack up your life to ride a little higher. Past the misery
house blowing leaves into misty hedges. The dusty winds of
November closing the meat curtains of tomorrow.

CALL OF THE WILD

That's nice, I said, what kind of a name is Mildred. Gentle strength, she said. A bit marmalade on toast, I said. A bit cat and whiskers. Dusty wisdom of books, she said. Tea and crumpets, I said. Not really, she said. Beans and toast. She scooted closer. Snuggled down inside herself. Her pearly wisdoms. She scooted closer. Pitched a tent. The pang of the wild. They rang the buzzer. We chose each other. The hunt is over, I said.

HIGH & DRY

In my fair mind it is fair weather. Giant sunflowers you pick the
seeds from. Squirrels rascal up the trees. Children butterfly their
stomachs. But really it is lashing. Cats and dogs. Drunks sway in
the overhang at Zabka asking for loose change. The weather of
your mind is not always the weather outside. We are cave bears
on slippery red sofa. Wodka with apple juice from the prairies.
Blue lights coat the ceiling. We light up our insides to balance
the outside. You can shave yourself high and dry and still breathe
here. Oh Poland it is hard not to love you.

HUNGRY GHOSTS

I follow the white monkey (Biała Małpa) down the hole and into
the beer garden. Someone is swinging in a hammock. The sand
resembles a beach. Minus the ocean or sea. I slip off my shoes.
Welcome to Biała Małpa, they say. New World IPA, they say.
Hoppy as sea foam the hoppy foams before me. I doth partake.
Behold we do the handshakes. Very good. Then my secret name.
Very good. Someone smiles. Miles & miles of good smile. As
god now. Stop, I say. I do not understand, I say. I do not want to
become god. Too late, says nobody. I will not knock on doors,
I say. You've already knocked, says nobody. It is your own door,
they say. We foam another hoppy. What is your state, they ask. I
was too much liquid or maybe gas. I needed more solids. I moved
to Spain for the solids. Very good, they say. It is a good first step,
the solids, that is really something, but then you get used to it, &
you want something else. We are all hungry ghosts.

ACKNOWLEDGEMENTS

Thanks to the editors of the following magazines for featuring selections from *Dream Dust* (in sometimes different forms):

Ghost City Review, The Lincoln Review, Bath Magg, Blackbox Manifold, Sprung Formal, Exacting Clam, Queen Mob's Teahouse, Bruiser, Ligeia, Hobart, Talking about Strawberries All the Time

Thanks to Rob Mclennan for featuring some poems from *Dream Dust* in *Periodicities* for his series: Short Takes on the Prose Poem.

Most importantly, thank you to friends and family. Especially my lover and life partner, Ewa Rasała.

LAY OUT YOUR UNREST

.

www.ingramcontent.com/pod-product-compliance
Lightning Source LLC
LaVergne TN
LVHW041310080426
835510LV00009B/942